Revolutionizing
Faith

Revolutionizing Faith

John Arnott

Sovereign World

Sovereign World Ltd
PO Box 777
Tonbridge
Kent TN11 0ZS
England

All Scripture quotations are taken from the New International Version unless otherwise stated. Copyright © 1973, 1978 International Bible Society. Published by Hodder & Stoughton

Quotations marked NKJV are taken from the New King James Bible © Thomas Nelson Publishers Inc. Nashville, USA

ISBN 1 85240 330 6

The publishers aim to produce books which will help to extend and build up the Kingdom of God. We do not necessarily agree with every view expressed by the author, or with every interpretation of Scripture expressed. We expect each reader to make his/her judgment in the light of their own understanding of God's Word and in an attitude of Christian love and fellowship.

Cover design by CCD, www.ccdgroup.co.uk
Typeset by CRB Associates, Reepham, Norfolk
Printed in the United States of America

Contents

About the Author

An international speaker and teacher, John Arnott is known for his ministry of the Lord's forgiveness and mercy. He is the Senior Pastor of Toronto Airport Christian Fellowship, and the Director of both Partners in Harvest and Friends in Harvest. John also coordinates *Catch the Fire*, a weekly television program, and *Spread the Fire*, a bi-monthly magazine which is distributed around the world.

John attended Ontario Bible College before pursuing a varied and successful career in business. In 1980, while on a ministry trip to Indonesia, John responded to God's call on his life for full-time ministry. Experience as a businessman, husband, father and pastor, has given John a richly blended ministry of God's grace, healing and deliverance. He puts a special emphasis on teaching about the Father heart of God and this has impacted many people with God's life-changing love and grace.

John and his wife Carol live in Toronto and travel extensively while continuing to pastor the Toronto Airport Christian Fellowship. Since 1994 John and Carol have invested much time and energy imparting God's anointing to people in many different cities and nations. They are welcomed and loved wherever they go.

John has written a number of books including the best selling *The Importance of Forgiveness* in the "What Christians Should Know About . . ." series.

Chapter 1

Childlike Faith

It is quite a daunting task to attempt to write about the subject of faith. It is a huge topic, yet there is none more central and fundamental. Faith is the foundational building block of our Christian lives. It is what our walk with God is all about. The whole of the Christian life is about faith that works by love. It is not faith in *our* faith or faith in our abilities. It is nothing to do with our ability to believe. Faith is essentially being *childlike* before God, putting our trust in Him and then resting in that, expecting Him to do all that He has promised to do and living in hope, because that is what God has called us to.

1 John 5:4 says,

> *"... for everyone born of God overcomes the world. This is the victory that has overcome the world, even our faith. Who is it that overcomes the world? Only he who believes that Jesus is the Son of God."*

The Apostle John says that our faith in Jesus Christ has enabled us to "overcome" – past tense – the world. Today you can look in the mirror and tell yourself, "My faith has overcome the world, because my faith is in the Son of God, the Lord Jesus."

Faith is not something that we can "work up". It is a gift given to us by God when we come to believe in His Son Jesus – a gift given because of His great grace toward us. Understanding God's grace is critical to understanding how faith works.

The grace of God is often a hard concept for people to grasp, especially those who are just getting started in the Christian life. Our human nature tends to lead us to think of Christianity as a mere *religion*, instead of a *relationship* with a living God. Thinking of Christianity as a religion reduces it to a system of rules and regulations which are put in place and adhered to in order to satisfy an impersonal, perfectionist God in the sky. If you live like that for a long time then you will eventually get burnt out, and you'll be no closer to God than you were at the beginning.

Thousands of people the world over are burnt out on church and the kind of Christianity that completely misses the point. They are tired of trying to "make the grade" and failing. What I am writing about here is an entirely different entity. God wants us to embrace a divine romance with Him. Our loving Father who created us in His own image, longs to have intimate time with us. He is desperate to win back to Himself those whose hearts have gone cold. He won't force us to come to Him, but desires to woo us into His presence.

This is the mystery of God – the fact that One so infinitely powerful and awesome should so desire to win the hearts of His created beings and reveal His loveliness to us, so that we will desire Him for who He is, and not just what He can give us.

The result of following a "rules and regulations" oriented religion is always *self-effort*. It means that we continually try to aspire to impossible standards and consistently fail. It is ironic when the faith we need is given freely by God through Jesus Christ His Son to all who surrender their lives to Him. God has looked at us and said, "You know what, you'll never be good enough or perfect enough in your own strength to be reconciled to Me; your own ability will never get you there. I will have to do something about it Myself."

So God prepared a gift. The gift was God Himself, come to earth as a man to pay our debt by dying on the cross, shedding His blood for you and me. Jesus paid the price for our sins in order to offer us the free gift of salvation if we will trust in Him. All you have to do is accept this free gift of grace from God. The moment you do, you're in. The moment you accept the gift of God, it is yours. That moment is where the faith that I am talking about begins. That is the starting point.

God's grace is ours despite all the feelings of unworthiness that we have. Something inside of us is prone to say, "I don't deserve God's forgiveness. I've been so bad that I don't know how God could ever love me." Yet, the faith that God gives us, that helps us to trust in Him and rely on His love, still functions despite our thoughts of unworthiness. Despite our sense that somehow it's not a fair deal for God to be freely offering us salvation, His grace is given to us. In spite of our human tendency to rationalize everything, God has reached out to us, and each of us needs to learn to break through the man-made barriers we create and, like a child, take hold of all God has for us.

Faith means trust

The Greek word translated "faith" really means "trust". Having faith means that you are putting your trust in God. The word "faith" is one that society has distorted so that it has lost much of its true meaning. People ask, "What *faith* do you belong to?" really meaning "How can I label your set of beliefs?" This kind of thinking robs the word "faith" of its trust-relationship dynamic. It attempts once again to reduce a relationship with the Almighty Creator to a set of rules and parameters.

In the early days of the establishment of the Christian Church, when the Holy Spirit was first poured out upon men, the believers identified themselves as those who put their trust in God's ability, rather than their own self-effort. Are you getting this? We need to be reminded constantly of our reliance upon God, such is our propensity to trust in our own ability. We just have to go over it and over it and over it, because our tendency is to lapse back into living the Christian life in our own strength – setting rules for ourselves, trying to behave well, thinking that these things will earn us points with God.

It is amazing to me how God has ordained faith as the key to His kingdom. He wants us to be able to access all the treasures of His kingdom, purely and simply by faith. There are so many other aspects of the Christian life that we might expect to play a central part – praying fervently, meditating in His Word – but none of these things make us any better in God's sight, no matter how much we do them. Instead, God has ordained that all the privileges of knowing Him are accessed only by faith.

Carol and I minister at a lot of meetings and there have been times when we've felt ill-prepared. We've wished more than once that we'd been able to pray more or study more, or generally be better prepared. Inevitably there is a tendency to feel that if you prepare better, somehow God will show up in a bigger way; that we will "earn" the right to His presence. Occasionally there have been times when we were "super-prepared" for a meeting and thinking, "Boy, it's going to be a top meeting tonight" and the meeting was really flat. We were left thinking, "God, what happened?"

In all honesty, it took me a while to figure this out, but for a while I just thought, "Everything goes a lot better when I don't prepare at all." Eventually I realized that things simply go much better when you step back and allow God to come forward. During those times of weakness when you say, "O God, it will have to be you tonight Lord, because I just don't have anything to give" the Lord says, "Good. We'll have a great meeting." But even when we feel prepared and ready to give we must learn to surrender to Him and allow Him to do what He wants to do. I am slowly catching on to the fact that no matter how well-prepared you are, it has nothing to do with you earning points of favor with God and Him therefore releasing more blessing as a result.

God responds to faith not need

If you are going to be born again and go to heaven when you die, it will be because in childlike trust you laid hold of the offer that God was making and said, "I choose to believe that Jesus can save a wretch like me."

"A wretch like me." I love those words from the hymn *Amazing Grace*. It was written by a slave trader, John Newton who captained a slaver for many years. One day, in the midst of a tremendous storm, with his boat sinking, he was reading the New Testament and praying one of those desperate, "O God, O God, O God" prayers. God brought him through the storm and the sinking ship never hit the bottom, it remained floating just under the water line and drifted, eventually beaching on an island somewhere. Newton had prayed, "Lord, if you ever get me out of this I will give my life to you." The Lord raised him up to be an Anglican preacher and pastor and he eventually wrote those words,

Amazing Grace, how sweet the sound,
that saved a wretch like me.
I once was lost, but now am found,
was blind, but now I see.

What did Newton have to bring to the table in his negotiations with God? Nothing. Nothing, other than a willingness to surrender to God and accept the offer of His free gift. Isn't that a wonderful way to begin your life with God? None of us are too bad to come to God.

My friend Mike Murdoch once made what was to me at the time, an amazing statement. He said that God does not respond to need, He only ever responds to faith. When I heard that I said to myself, "Wow! Can that be true?" I began processing it, going through the Scriptures and going through it in my mind, and I thought about it for a whole six months before deciding that it was absolutely true. If God would respond to need, there would be no street children being shot down in Brazil right now. If God responded to need, there would be no sin in the world. It is actually impossible for God to simply respond to need, because it would inevitably involve taking away the free will of man.

Each of us have to take responsibility for the mess we are in. It is not God's heart and it is not God's fault that we are the way we are. Your sin and mine has caused the mess that we are in. God is the one who all day long is stretching out His hands saying, *"Come to me, all you who are weary and burdened, and I will give you rest"* (Matthew 11:28).

God is not responsible for the sins of the human race, yet His solution for the messes that we get ourselves into can be accessed by putting our faith in Him and bringing the Kingdom of God into those situations. When Jesus walked this earth, wherever He went, He was bringing the Kingdom of God by faith into the here and now. That is what you and I are called to do too. We can appropriate God's offer, by choosing to trust in Him.

God knows our needs

I want to pose a question. What do you need today? What are you praying about at the moment? What do you need from God? Do you need money to see your ministry go ahead? Do you need friends? Do you need a better job? Do you need more power in your church? Do you need more prayer happening in your church? Do you want to see more blessing upon your kids and upon your family and everything else?

Do you think you need to be continually on your knees telling God about those things? You know what? He already knows about them. These things are accessed by a simple, childlike trust in the nature of God. God already knows all our needs. What He wants more than anything is for us to trust – i.e. have faith – in Him, that He knows about those needs and has promised to provide for them because we are His children. The point at which you realize this is the point where you can fall back into His arms and say, "I know that these things are mine in the name of Jesus." It is not an issue of presumption – that we arrogantly expect God to give us every-thing we *want*. We pray as the Spirit leads us, knowing that we have need of something and know-ing that God will provide for that need, then we trust Him for it. That is truly appropriating the promises of God. All your needs in this life are met through faith – food, shelter, health, healing, needs for your children, etc. You will only receive these things by putting your faith, and therefore your trust, in the Father's love. Do you think you could do that today?

Jesus asked the question of His disciples, "What is the matter with you? Don't you know the Father cares for the grass? Don't you know He cares for the sparrows? Don't you know that He has even numbered the hairs on your head? What are you so worried about? Why are you so fearful, O ye of little faith! Put your trust in God who is able to take care of you from the day that you were born until the day of your last breath." (See Matthew 6:25–34.)

Take all those issues in your life to God today,

either on your own before Him, or with a friend, or with your husband or your wife, and pray and declare before God, "I am going to put my trust in You today Lord." I don't care how bad it looks, He is not limited by circumstances. Put your trust in Him now. God wants you to get a handle on any anxiety that is in your heart right now. What things are you anxious about? The Father wants you to put your hope in Him. If you put your trust in Him like a little child He will see you through. Jesus taught us that it is those who are like children that will be able to enter and enjoy God's Kingdom.

Being able to enter into the things of God's Kingdom in a childlike way means that you won't necessarily always understand everything. How many of us are prepared to allow that to happen, to be vulnerable enough to say "God is God and how He chooses to work in my life is His business. He loves me and He will always take care of me." If you need to understand everything that God does, then you are going to miss the benefits of living in His Kingdom. Are you willing to leave some things totally in His hands? How about leaving *everything* to Him? Having a relationship with God is not intended to be a mental exercise. God gave us highly intelligent minds and we can use them as He intended, but let us never allow our minds to come between us and God! God never intended for it to be hard to receive His promises; it's simple, which is why Jesus stressed the need for childlikeness.

Persisting to bear fruit

All of us who are believers hope to live fruitful, productive Christian lives. I am talking about going beyond just staying saved and getting into heaven. I am talking about wanting God to use you, so that one day you will be able to enter His presence with numerous other souls that you played a part in bringing to Him. Most of us want to have a measure of such "success" in our Christian lives, but the only way that we will bear significant fruit and see those things happen is by taking hold of them in Spirit-led prayer and trusting God to see them come to pass.

Sometimes it is a battle to continue in childlike faith. The devil will constantly put hurdles in your way and try to make you believe it's more complicated than you originally thought. In those times you need to declare to the enemy the truth that he is defeated and order him to get under your feet. There will be circumstances in life that will hinder you, people that won't like what they perceive as your "over simplistic" faith, who will disagree with you and obstruct you. All of that has to be put out of the way.

The biblical example of Elisha and Elijah provides us with an excellent model for simple, persistent, childlike faith that is determined to lay hold of the promises of God. Elisha knew that it was his destiny to succeed his master Elijah as the prophet of God in the land. The Lord must have revealed to Elisha that Elijah was about to die, for he seemed to be aware that he must "hold on" to Elijah at all costs, yet Elisha was being hindered during the succession process. Elijah himself was trying to get Elisha to stay behind whilst he went alone to Bethel, but Elisha refused to allow his "promise" out of his sight! He refused to allow his inheritance to simply disappear: *"As surely as the Lord lives and as you live, I will not leave you"* he insisted (2 Kings 2:4).

Elijah attempted one more time to leave Elisha behind before he finally relented and asked, *"Tell me, what can I do for you before I am taken from you?"* Elisha replied, *"Let me inherit a double portion of your spirit."*

Elisha had decided that, come what may, he was going to stick with it and persist until he saw the fulfillment of God's promise in his life. Elijah responded to him, saying that he had asked a very difficult thing, but nevertheless, if Elisha saw him at the moment when God took him from the earth, his request would be granted.

Elisha did receive his anointing and became the prophet of God. He took hold of it by childlike, persistent, dogged, holding-on-until-the-bitter-end faith. He was not going to take no for an answer. God had promised it to him and he was going for it with everything he had. All of your needs are met like this too – by the ability to lay hold of God and trust Him.

Faith depends on the power of God

I want to make it clear that I am not talking about

blind faith here, or a naivete which is disconnected from reality. We can trust in God, not because of any power that we possess, but simply because of the great and awesome power that He possesses. The presence and power of God is real and tangible. It is understanding God's all-sufficiency and power that should convince you and help you to reach out and take hold of Him in trust.

In 1 Corinthians 2:4–5 Paul says,

"My message and my preaching were not with wise and persuasive words, but with a demonstration of the Spirit's power, so that your faith might not rest on men's wisdom, but on God's power."

What a wonderful verse that is! Although Paul was a highly educated man and could no doubt have provided a compelling intellectual argument for the Gospel, he refused to rely on the wisdom of men, submitting instead to the Holy Spirit and allowing the power of God to be displayed. Why? So that his converts' faith would be based upon God's power rather than intellectual beliefs.

When people see the power of God manifested, there is a conviction that comes upon them that is supernatural. They are not "convinced" by clever speeches or compelling arguments, but they are gripped by the power of the Spirit in a way that utterly convinces them of the power of God. Whenever we have had miracles in our meetings, people have always responded to the altar call. They see something that really hits them and they say, "Wow! God is really here." People who were skeptical and unconvinced before, suddenly get convinced when they see a powerful demonstration of the Spirit.

"Laying hold" by faith

Everything you have you possess because of laying hold of it by faith. God drops a little seed of an idea into your heart and you say, "Lord, can it be?" He says, "Yes, it can be" and you begin to believe and you begin to take action. I'll never forget when we bought the building that now houses our church. We were so frustrated in our tiny building and spent virtually the whole of 1994 moving in and out of local banquet halls that were large enough to hold all the people that were coming to the meetings. Thousands of people were coming and we prayed, "Oh God, please give us a bigger place! Please make it easy because we don't have time to build something that might take three years."

Not long after that a potential building dropped right in our lap. At first all we could say was, "Wow! Is this it?", then we buckled on our faith and decided to go for it. We put in an offer on the building, but it was rejected. The owners accepted another offer from a Hong Kong based group and it became the Asian Trade Center. I couldn't believe it because I was convinced that this was *our* building. They put their sign up outside and every time I drove by it I would just about throw up! "Oh God, what now?" I wanted to know, but the Lord simply said, "Trust Me." I would protest and say, "Yes, but ..." but the answer was always the same: "Trust Me." Have you ever been there?

Naturally we began to think about other options. We thought about ways in which we could expand our old building and spent hundreds of hours weighing up the alternatives. All the while our major Prophetic Conference was looming and we knew that, once again, thousands of visitors would be arriving. Not long before the conference, the local hotel called us to say that there were so many people registered that they couldn't hold them all, and asked if we would be open to having the conference in an off-site rented auditorium? They suggested the Attwell Center. This was a surprise to us because we thought it was closed, but they seemed positive that they could get it. Well, we moved into the Attwell Center and you know what? We never moved out! How did that happen?

I remember walking around the place with Wes Campbell. All the time he was saying to me, "This is the place bro. Go for it, put a deposit on it" and I was saying, "Take it easy Wes, we're trying to hear God here. How do you buy a $2.2 million building?" The situation was this: the Attwell Center was a $9 million building. We were buying it for $2.2 million and the owners wanted a $1 million deposit and we didn't have any money. It looked totally impossible, but that's the business we are in isn't it? In the end we just decided that we would take all our chips, push them into the center of the table, bet the whole deal on the Lord Jesus Christ, and wait to see what He would do.

It is at this point in life that you have really got to watch it. You cannot operate from a position of presumption. You must know that you have heard from God. If it turns out to be just your own idea and not His idea, then you will sink like a stone. But I can assure you that when you catch the heart of God and you see the needs of people and your motives are right, you can latch on to Him in faith and things will come to pass.

What is your dream? Do you want to go and do something for Jesus? Do you want to be a history maker – a world changer? That dream to do something great for God's kingdom inside of you has been put there by Him. It is stirred up by the Holy Spirit. The way you take hold of it is through faith – through a childlike trust in obedience to God. Every one of us has to come to the place where we are prepared to count the cost and lay hold of that dream. We have to say to ourselves, "I am going for this. If I lose everything, then I lose everything, but I am going for this for the Kingdom of God."

I once met a lady who was married to a Jewish man who was not a born-again believer. For years and years she had just put up with his objections to her faith. He would regularly say things like, "Will you turn that program off" or, "Get rid of that Bible." One day however, he was diagnosed with cancer and had to be admitted to hospital for surgery on a tumor. It's ironic how someone in that position will suddenly become open to prayer. When you are at that point, you will take anything that might work. His wife and others prayed for him and when the doctors examined him prior to the operation they said, "We don't understand it. There is no tumor. It's completely disappeared!" That miracle so impressed the man that he became totally open to things that he had never been open to before. Why? Because the power of God is a *demonstration* that these things are real and we access them by laying hold of them by faith.

Faith that can move mountains

1 Corinthians 13:2 speaks of a faith that can *"... move mountains ... "*. Have you got any mountains in your life that you would like to move? The scripture goes on to say that despite having such faith, if you don't have love, then you don't have anything. That is why it is so important that you and I have a foundation of love beneath us that is the bedrock of our faith.

God so loved the world, so loved you, that He gave his only Son to die in your place, paying the price for your sins. The only appropriate response to that is, "Lord you have so loved me, therefore fill my heart so that I can love other people. I don't want to be a taker,

I want to be a giver." There are two kinds of people in this world – givers and takers. God has called us to be givers. Our aim should be to say to God, "I don't know how this is going to come out, but I am going to be a giver. I am going to give my time, my energy, my money to God and believe Him that something good is going to come out."

Walking by faith and not by sight

Paul also says in 2 Corinthians 5:7 that we walk by *faith* and not by *sight*. What does that mean? It means that to walk with God we don't rely on our own smarts. We don't rely on our ability to be street-wise and shrewd. Instead we are constantly listening for the gentle voice of the Holy Spirit, lovingly speaking to us, "This is the way. Walk *this* way." When you believe God is speaking to you like that, it is perfectly OK to check it out with the Word of God, and with trusted friends, but as God leads us, that's how we walk by faith.

Faith is God's method for accessing everything in His Kingdom – all of His heavenly resources. Human wisdom cannot achieve it, only childlike faith. Everything you need in your Christian life will come to you by faith. That is what Jesus said to the sick man in Matthew 9:29: *"According to your faith, be it unto you."* That is why it is so important that you don't allow your faith to be diluted and weakened by fear, or unbelief. If you allow fear and insecurity to rule your life then you will find it difficult to exercise your faith as you should. Fear is *negative faith.* It is contrary to faith. The Bible says that whatever is not of faith is sin.

If you feel that fear has dominated you, then get some trusted friends around you to pray about it today. If it helps, write down all the things that you are facing in your life right now – any uncertainties, worries or problems. Get them out in the light and identify them clearly before the Father. What are you afraid of? What is the worst case scenario in life for you? What do you need from God today? What is it that you are always praying about? What are the miracles you are believing for? When you have the list in front of you, offer it up to the Father and pray,

> "Lord I put all my fears aside and trust you completely. I lay aside all the guilt and shame of the past and put my faith in you. I surrender all these things that I have written about into Your hands now. Today I am going forward in faith, trusting in You, in Jesus' name. Amen."

As you purpose to do that, you are saying, "God I am going to believe you for these miracles that I need." Hebrews 6:12 says that the saints through *"faith and patience"* inherited the promises of God. Seeing your miracle come to pass will take two things – faith and time. Sometimes God will move in an instant, and other times you will need faith and patience. But when God gives you a promise, you can bet on His faithfulness.

Chapter 2

The Subject of Faith

Faith is an interesting ingredient. The Bible speaks of faith as being both a *gift* of the Spirit and also a *fruit* of the Spirit. All of us desire to believe God for things in a childlike way, without striving or gritting our teeth, trying to make something happen. To do that we need an impartation of faith from the Holy Spirit – it comes as a gift and reveals itself as fruit in our lives as we exercise that gift.

In the previous chapter I made the statement, "God responds to faith and not need" – a statement which some may find provoking. I would qualify that statement by saying, clearly God is not ignorant of our needs, but desires us to come to Him in expectancy. God saw the desperate plight of humanity and responded to our great need for a savior by sending His own Son, Jesus Christ to save us. That was God's initiative. Regarding our individual, personal needs apart from salvation, God looks for us to express our faith and trust in Him to meet our needs. God sees your need, but He has established faith as the means by which your need is fulfilled.

Putting your trust in God is not an excuse to sit back and say, "I can just leave everything up to God. I don't need to do a thing." No, it is a process whereby we listen to God speaking to our heart, prompting us to pray about specific needs, and then partner with Him in order to see those things come to pass.

God is committed to meeting our needs, but He often does so indirectly. For the most part, He wants to meet them through your brothers and sisters in Christ. Isn't that amazing? Generally speaking, He doesn't send the angels to do it, nor does He come down Himself and do it directly, but He wants to meet your needs primarily through others in the Body of Christ as they hear His heart and move out in faith. This is the Body functioning as it should.

Think about the nation of Israel. God's people in bondage to Egypt needed a deliverer. God saw their need. Did He go in and deal with it directly? No, He raised up Moses and called him to be the one who would carry the presence of God to deliver the nation.

God wants to partner with you

Some of this is bewildering to me. Why does God want to partner with you and me? Why does He want to partner with human beings in order to fulfill His will? In part, I think the reason is that He wants

Spirit-filled men and women to be the ones executing His plan of action to rescue those who are far away from Him. God is looking for people who will say "Yes" to Him and will partner with Him to change the face of humanity.

Although God used Moses to deliver an entire nation, notice how reluctant Moses was to get involved. Moses heard the Lord speaking to Him from a burning bush. Realizing the enormity of God's call upon him, everything in him was yelling, "Oh God, please just use somebody else!" Have you ever felt like that? "Do I really have to do this God? Can't you send somebody else. Isn't there another way?" It's a common reaction. Every one of us has said or felt it at some time. Why? Because compared to our limited human way of thinking, God thinks big! The projects He embarks upon look impossible to us. In fact, they usually are impossible – for us. They are always too big for us to tackle alone, which is how God wants it. This is part and parcel of the walk of faith.

Moses wanted to know from God how he could just walk up to Pharaoh and say, "The One whose name is 'I Am' says, 'Let My people go.'" He could already imagine Pharaoh saying, "I don't know this God. Why should I let the people go?" So the Lord gave Moses some signs to convince the Pharaoh that he was for real – the leprous hand that miraculously became clean again in front of Pharaoh's eyes, and the staff that could turn into a snake. When Moses and Pharaoh finally met, Pharaoh was not impressed with these signs. "My magicians can do the same thing," he said. Moses must have thought, "Oh Lord, this is not working." But as he walked through the plan that God had laid out, step by step, he got to witness first-hand the mighty, delivering hand of God as He freed Israel from slavery.

It is incredible how faith works. You hear God calling you to do something utterly impossible and think, "How can that ever be?" Yet, step by step He walks you through His preordained plan and the impossible comes to pass.

Moses had every excuse in the book why he couldn't do what God was asking him to do. "God I can't speak, I have a bad stutter, you know I am not one of those dynamic communicators. Can't You use somebody else?" The Lord almost got angry with him. He said,

"Who gave man his mouth? Who makes him deaf or mute? Who gives him sight or makes him blind? Is it not I, the LORD*? Now go; I will help you speak and will teach you what to say."*   (Exodus 4:11–12)

Think about what excuses you might be making to the Lord in your heart. Is He calling you to do something for Him, or to believe for a miracle in your life? What are you saying back to Him? "I'm too old ... I'm too young ... I don't have the education ... I don't have what it takes ... I don't have influence ... " All those statements are designed to *disqualify* us from doing the will of God, just as Moses tried to say that he wasn't qualified to do what God wanted him to do. Do you know what they really are? They are lies planted in your heart. Say to yourself, "Nothing is impossible with God." This is the truth! Every step of the way He will be with you. Whatever life presents to you, you can say, "Well Lord, here is another challenge. I wonder what you are going to do with this one?" Moses had to walk through that process and so can you.

Authentic faith = simple obedience

At the beginning of Acts 2 we see Jesus' disciples gathered together, waiting for the promise of the Father that Jesus gave them in Acts 1. We need to speculate about what that must have been like for them. They were commanded by Jesus, *"Do not leave Jerusalem, but wait for the gift my Father promised ... in a few days you will be baptized with the Holy Spirit"* (Acts 1:4–5). God's message to us is the same. When He calls and appoints us to do something for Him, we must not run off and try to accomplish it in the flesh – according to our own wisdom, effort or resources. God wants to partner with us in the endeavor and will fill us with His Holy Spirit so that we will be empowered for the task.

On the day of Pentecost, the disciples were in the upper room, waiting and praying simply because that is what God had told them to do. They were responding to His command to wait until they were empowered. Do you see that that was authentic faith? They weren't trying to make it happen themselves, they were not striving, they were not trying to earn the right to be blessed by God. Authentic faith = simple obedience. Faith is obediently responding to God's request. If He tells you to go, then you go and He will empower you. If He tells you to wait and pray, then you wait and pray and He will empower you!

Ultimately, the disciples were able to testify in Acts 2, "The Holy Spirit fell upon us." Their testimony brought glory to God because it wasn't anything they did. They didn't pray it down; it wasn't because they were "holy enough" or "good enough"; it wasn't because they worked for it. They responded in simple obedience and after they were filled with the Holy Spirit they became very, very effective in fulfilling the Great Commission and extending God's Kingdom.

Simple steps of faith

I believe that it is up to us to welcome God's provision. I don't believe in a works-based religious system, but I believe in one where we respond to the Lord's initiative. God wants to fill you with the Holy Spirit; He wants to equip you with the gifts of the Spirit and with faith, miracles and signs and wonders. All that is required of you is to say, "Yes Lord, I want to receive those things from You."

When God asks us to do something for Him,

although the entire project may be enormous, probably impossible in our eyes, the first step He requires us to take is usually a simple one. "Wait and pray ..." "Say to Pharaoh, 'Let My people go.'" God gives us simple instructions. The age-old human problem is that so often we respond by saying, "It can't be that simple Lord." Moses objected to the Lord's plan, saying in effect, "Don't you realize that Pharaoh is the leader of the most powerful nation on earth? I can't just walk up to him and say that. It's not that simple." That is where childlike trust comes in. When God gives you something to do, just purpose in your heart to do it. It will be something simple. Once you take that step there will be another simple step to take. You learn by taking one step after the next. That's how to learn to walk in faith.

I remember the time when Carol and I were called to go to Argentina. We came up with at least a dozen practical reasons why we shouldn't go. All we felt was this prompting of the Lord to "go". "Just go" was what He said to us. "But Lord," I protested, "It's going to cost us everything we've got in our savings account." "I know," He replied, "But just go." Thank God we did go in the end, because it revolutionized our lives. I sometimes pause to think where we would be now if we hadn't gone. We came home from there with such a fresh impartation of the Holy Spirit that soon exploded in our church. It was so, so good, and to think that we could have so easily missed it. God was gently calling and leading us and we were so unsure and hesitant, but in the end we obeyed. That obedience brought huge rewards. That is what faith is all about.

We need to be really careful when we come to those crossroads in life. Many times we don't recognize them for what they are – a critical moment in our walk with God. We had been on lots of trips all over the world. This looked like just one more trip. Should we go or shouldn't we? Little did we know that the destiny of God was riding on that trip. I am so thankful to the Lord Jesus that He impressed upon us to go. I am so thankful for every person around us who urged us to go in one way or another. I am so thankful that God met with us there in a mighty, mighty way. Again, it was through people – God's people in Argentina – that we were touched. It was God responding to human need through the Body of Christ.

Sometimes responding to God is going to cost you everything. Do you ever feel like you are having to risk everything in order to obey God? My friend Melinda Fish said that when she saw the hand that God was dealing her, she pushed all her poker chips to the center of the table! What "hand" was she talking about? When you see that God is dealing you the opportunity to be a partaker and a partner with Him in the things of the Spirit. When God speaks to you like that, I want you to bet everything in your life – past, present and future – on the Kingdom of God. Bet the whole thing on God and you will never lose. I am not talking about the kind of presumption where you do the initiating and come up with your own Kingdom-building plan – that's not the same. But, when God initiates something and invites you to come and be a part of it, working alongside Him, it makes all the difference in the world and you can stake your life on it.

Only Believe

I think it is impossible to be full of the Holy Spirit and full of bitterness, negativity and criticism at the same time. If you meet someone who claims to be full of the Spirit, but you hear bitterness, criticism, and negativity all the time, you can be sure that's not the Holy Spirit, but another spirit. That is the accuser rising up in them. The Holy Spirit is full of faith and when He fills you, your whole world changes. All of a sudden everybody is nice, the sky is bluer, the grass is greener, everything is wonderful.

One of my heroes from years gone, Smith Wigglesworth who was known as the "apostle of faith", had a favorite saying that he used over and again in his meetings. It was "Only believe." In other words, just simply trust Him – "only believe". When you come into line with the heart of the Father, you stop being critical and down on everything and you start being filled up with the love of Jesus. When that happens you start blessing everyone around you, forgiving those who have hurt you, repenting of your

sins – sometimes publicly – and you become free. Do
you know that you too can have this? Only believe
and that freedom can be yours. This is the blessing
and the promise of God.

The Bible uses a phrase to describe laying hold of
the promises of God and applying them to your life. It
says that you must *appropriate* them. What does that
mean? It is not a mystical term that we can't understand. It simply means to trust what God says is true
and to act upon it now.

Christine, a lady in our church, had been ill and
confined to a wheelchair for twelve years. Her
husband Frank had to carry her around everywhere
they went. They were not easy years for them as a
couple. They did everything they knew how to do –
prayed, fasted, sought the Lord – and nothing seemed
to be changing. But one day, as Chris was listening to
a praise and worship CD, the Lord whispered to her
and said, "I am going to heal you." She laid hold of
that promise by faith and began to believe. A few
months went by and she began to see little signs of
improvement like, "Wow! I can feel the blankets on
my feet. Something is changing." She laid hold of the
word God spoke to her by faith and eventually
ditched that wheelchair completely. She has been
walking around without it for about ten years now!

Justification by faith in Christ

Romans 3:21–24 says,

"But now a righteousness from God, apart from law, has been made known, to which the Law and the Prophets testify. This righteousness from God comes through faith in Jesus Christ to all who believe. There is no difference, for all have sinned and fall short of the glory of God, and are justified freely by His grace through the redemption that came by Christ Jesus."

Paul taught that each of us has an equal standing before God. There is nothing to distinguish a Jew who keeps the law from a Gentile before God. All that counts is whether or not a person trusts in Christ as his Savior. Through faith (simply trusting in Jesus), there is no difference at all. Everyone and anyone can approach the Lord.

God didn't sweep your sin under the carpet and say, "Oh well, let's forget about that, it doesn't matter." Sin matters very, very much. Sin is when we do our thing, usually at the expense of someone else, and we don't care about them because we want to do *our thing.* God calls it sin. God knew all about mankind's sin and He could not just ignore it, so He came up with a scheme whereby His Son, Jesus, would pay the price for our sin by dying on the cross. Jesus therefore, is the one to justify us before God as we put our faith in Him. This offer of salvation through faith alone was, and is, offered to mankind as a free gift of God.

Romans 5:1–2 says,

"Therefore, since we have been justified through faith,

*we have peace with God through our Lord Jesus Christ,
through whom we have gained access by faith into this
grace in which we now stand."*

We have peace with God through our faith in
Jesus. That's how it begins and that's how it continues
for you and me in our Christian lives.

Trusting, not striving

Romans 9:30–31 says,

*"... the Gentiles, who did not pursue righteousness,
have obtained it, a righteousness that is by faith; but
Israel, who pursued a law of righteousness, has not
attained it. Why not? Because they pursued it not by
faith but as if it were by works. They stumbled over
the 'stumbling stone'."*

Why did Paul accuse Israel of unbelief in this letter
to the Romans? Because, he says, they saw righteousness as something to be attained by works. They did
not seek righteousness by faith. They stumbled at the
"stumbling stone" – Jesus – and they didn't get what
He was saying. Jesus came to show us that it is *only*
through faith in Him that we can attain righteousness.
Israel, who were pursuing righteousness through self-
effort, self-discipline, and trying desperately to keep all
the commandments, missed it. Religion totally missed
the point and religion will always miss it.

Israel missed it because they thought that "good works" was what it takes to secure salvation. The Christian gospel has now been heard for 2,000 years, and you would think that the major denominations of our faith would have learnt and understood the fundamentals of it by now. "The just shall live by faith", yet that is not what they do. People continually fall into the trap of thinking that *what they do* will save them. They strive to please God. It is not about that. The Christian life is about having a love relationship with the Father that you receive by faith.

Again the Apostle Paul proclaims to us,

> *"... what does it say? 'The word is near you; it is in your mouth and in your heart,' that is, the word of faith we are proclaiming: That if you confess with your mouth, 'Jesus is Lord,' and believe in your heart that God raised him from the dead, you will be saved. For it is with your heart that you believe and are justified, and it is with your mouth that you confess and are saved."* (Romans 10:8–10)

Paul says, "This is the word of faith we are preaching," or in other words, "The message of trust we are trusting." It's that simple he insists. Confess with your mouth and believe with your heart. Trust Jesus and you will be saved. Trust in Jesus and your life will be revolutionized. The word is trust. That is how you receive grace or gifts – you take them by faith.

My prayer is that by reading this short book you

will be encouraged to trust Him more. Not with anxiety, not with striving, but resting in Him with an assurance that your loving, heavenly Father is watching over you. I am not asking you to step up to bat for a faith that's based on working to *deserve* God's grace, but one that encourages you to fall into the everlasting arms of God, like a child would run and leap into their parent's arms; a faith that encourages you to step into the provision that the Father has promised to you. Choose to say, "I trust you Father. I am not going to try to make things happen, but I am going to respond to whatever you tell me to do." Then let the peace of God rule in your hearts. Keep reminding yourself that you are not trying to live in your own strength. You have a different assignment. Fall in love with your Savior. Allow Him to fill you with His Spirit and meet your every need. Read the Word of God. Talk to Him and let Him talk back to you, heart to heart. That is a living, real faith.

Chapter 3

Have Faith in ...

True success

I believe that every one of us would desire to enter into a greater level of faith, where our walk with God became so much more than merely a theological concept. We desire to be *successful* in our walk with God, and *successful* in terms of our effectiveness for Him.

You may long to walk more deeply in God's love. You may desire a deeper love for the Word of God. Perhaps you yearn to move in your gifting under the anointing of the Holy Spirit in a greater way than ever before. Perhaps you desire to learn how to defeat the enemy more often so that your life does not consist of one failure after another, with the enemy abusing and defeating you. You know that it is possible to be more than a conqueror through Him who loves you and you want to live there.

This is the kind of "success" I am thinking of, and all these things *are possible* by appropriating them through childlike trust in the awesome Person of God. There are three areas I will touch on in this final chapter that I hope will encourage you to see that this is true.

1. You can have faith in His Word

We can rest assured of the total reliability of the Bible – the infallible Word of God – and believe wholeheartedly in all that it says is true of us as believers. Written by so many different authors, yet never contradictory, numerous scholars have scrutinized and criticized it through the years, but it has stood the test of time. If you are tuned in to the heart of the Father then you will follow this book because it is a book of life. It is a book that will bless you, guide and keep you. Let us consider what the Bible says about itself:

> *"For the word of God is living and active. Sharper than any double-edged sword, it penetrates even to dividing soul and spirit, joints and marrow; it judges the thoughts and attitudes of the heart."*
> (Hebrews 4:12)

This book is alive! It is not a dead book. You might wonder about that when you are struggling through the Book of Leviticus perhaps, but from beginning to end it is absolutely full of life. There are multiplied millions of people throughout history who have purposed in their heart to follow the teachings of this book, and as they have done so, have found their lives begin to become productive. Their lives have become successful. A relationship with God has become a reality because of the life-imparting power of this book. I have also seen people shipwreck their lives when they have deviated from following the teachings of the Word. A life can be ruined in just one weekend of rebellion. You can set yourself back years by disobeying God's Word.

But for those who say, "I am going to believe in God's Word. I am going to read it and treasure it. I am going to put my confidence in the Word and follow its teachings" – for them, goodness and mercy follow them all their lives; blessing follows them around wherever they go.

The Word is a weapon

The Bible describes itself as sharper than any two-edged sword. Jesus knew this very well and handled the Word as such. He used the Word as a weapon to defeat the enemy as the account in Matthew's gospel reveals.

"Then Jesus was led by the Spirit into the desert to be tempted by the devil ... The tempter came to him and said, 'If you are the Son of God, tell these stones to become bread.' Jesus answered, 'It is written; "Man

does not live on bread alone, but on every word that
comes from the mouth of God."'" (Matthew 4:2–4)

Three times Jesus responded to the devil's attack
by saying, *"It is written . . . "* The weapon of the Word
in Jesus' hands was effective in defeating him.

While He was on earth, Jesus never once operated
from His divine nature. He chose to set aside His
divine authority in favor of operating purely as a
man filled with the power of the Holy Spirit. That's
why He preferred to be called the Son of Man. He
chose to be tested and tempted in every way, just as
we are, and triumphed by remaining sinless.

Similarly, as Jesus relied on "every word" that
came from God, we too can rely on every "word" that
the Father speaks to us and put our faith in what He
says. You may know in your heart that God has
spoken to you about ministering to young people, or
about planting churches, or about being a prophet to
the Body of Christ, or about being a musician. The
devil may come to you and say, "If God has called you
to that, then why don't you prove it?" He will delight
in suggesting to you that you should do this or that in
order to try and "make" the will of God happen – just
as He did with Jesus. Jesus simply spoke back the
Word in defense. He knew that the devil was a liar and
refused to rise to his enticements. In these moments
we can speak out the truth of God's word to us. We
can declare what we know is "true" about us according to God's Word and what His will is for our lives.

Next time the devil comes along whispering lies about how you are good for nothing and that you are not much of a Christian, that God doesn't love you or even see you, or care about you, then you need to stand up on the inside and resist him and quote him a verse of scripture like Jesus did. You can successfully contest the lies of the enemy with the truth of what the Word of God says.

Aligning yourself with the truth

We can learn more from Jesus' response than just how to deal with the enemy. It was characteristic of Jesus never to rise to calls to prove Himself to anyone. Likewise, we don't have to fall into the trap of proving ourselves to other people. Instead we can rest in the knowledge that we have a loving, heavenly Father who has called forth our life for a specific purpose which He will bring to pass as we co-operate with Him. This is what Jesus did time after time.

Our friends Chester and Betsy Kylstra often minister at our church in the area of inner healing and deliverance. They ministered to our senior leadership team some time ago and we were all amazed to discover that there were still some lies of the enemy lurking in our hearts. Each of us was burdened with untrue things that we believed – things that said we could never become the person God purposed us to be, or do the things He planned for us to do. All of these lies were in complete contradiction to the Word of God.

The Kylstra's method of ministry is to compare what the Bible says is true about you to the beliefs that you actually hold. Sometimes you don't always realize that you have ungodly beliefs, but your actions and the way that you behave can reveal them. Chester and Betsy encourage you to confess the truths of the Bible and to speak life deep into your spirit. The truth of God's Word begins to counteract the ungodly beliefs and set you free.

Having faith in the Word of God is not just about defeating the enemy, although it is all of that. It calls us to a higher place – to have faith that we can enter a more intimate realm of walking with God in the power of the Holy Spirit. Often we don't feel that we deserve to enjoy such fullness in Christ. We don't feel qualified. This is something quite separate from the tempting and testing of the enemy. It arises from our human inability to realize the momentous power of Him who dwells within us and all that He desires to give us. We find it so difficult to come to terms with the fact that humanly speaking, you can be the biggest zero in the world, yet when Christ lives in you and begins moving through you, miracles and supernatural things can and will happen.

Moses spent forty years in the desert looking after sheep. Humanly speaking he would never have picked himself as the one to lead a nation of slaves out of bondage. Actually, Moses did not have much going for him at all – except this one thing: God was with him. We also need to remind ourselves that God is with us. We are not alone! He is continually with us. You need to know that *you* are more than a conqueror through Him who loves you.

Statements like that are not simply charismatic clichés. I am not advocating the kind of spiritual hype where you make declarations over and again until you convince yourself that you believe them. However, truths such as the one above have to be appropriated simply, by faith. You declare the truth of the Word and trust God to fulfill that truth in your life.

Even if you feel today that you are not worth much, doesn't God delight in taking the simple things – things that are maybe looked down upon and despised by others, things that don't amount to much, and use them for His honor and glory? God loves to do that so that no-one can say, "God used me because I was smart ... talented ... skilled ... " etc. God often picks those less likely to succeed and then confounds the world by doing miracles through them.

I love to remind myself that everything in life begins with a thought. Great endeavors usually begin with a dream. If you are so disillusioned that you don't dream anymore, then you need your heart healed, because God wants to fill us with visions and dreams. Why is that? Because everything flows out of it. The bed you sleep in, the clothes you wear, the house you live in, all began as thoughts – dreams inside the mind of a designer.

God wants to give you godly dreams – dreams

about things you will achieve for Him. The enemy of course wants to rob you of those dreams, because he knows that will hinder and stifle your purpose in God. It's then that you need to know the Word of God. I urge everyone, don't let a day go by without spending time in the Word of God, because that way you will store up great "reserves" of truth in your heart, ready to defeat the enemy with when he comes calling.

2. You can have faith in His love

I come across so many people who have become disillusioned with God for some reason or other. Actually, they are mostly disillusioned with the Church and other Christians rather than God, but God usually gets the blame. I once interviewed a young man who was seeking to get back into the ministry after a long time away. Things had not gone right in his life and he got so mad at God about it. He told me that he turned on God, swore at Him and just backslid. Now, having come back to God, he was struggling with the question, "Will God have me back?" Of course God would and did have Him back. When the Father sees a repentant or broken heart, His response is always, "Yes, I'll take you back. Come on, come to Me now!" God is so merciful.

Do you have faith in God and His wonderful Father-heart for you? He just wants to gather you up in His arms. He is always whispering to you, "Come closer. Draw close to Me." He draws us to Himself. He longs for us to respond in faith and believe in His great and awesome love for us.

God is *so* loving. After being a Christian for many years, my only regret is that for most of that time I didn't know how nice God was. I was in pursuit of the truth and I didn't know it was all about love. The love of God is the absolute foundation of our lives. I had a *theology* of the love of God, I knew the Bible *talked about* the love of God, but it hadn't really penetrated my heart so that I *knew* love was the foundational thing, and that everything else must be built on that.

If the foundation of your faith is built on anything other than love, then you are going to end up in religion. What motivates your Christian faith? Are you driven by a pursuit of truth? You'll become a Pharisee. Are you driven by achieving, working hard for God? You will become a hardened striver that injures people all around you. If you are driven by anything else but the love and the heart of God, you are going to miss the mark, because this is the central, foundational thing. Everything else flows from it.

In Romans 5:5 we read,

"And hope does not disappoint us, because God has poured out his love into our hearts by the Holy Spirit, whom he has given us."

Picture yourself standing with a big funnel over the top of you. The funnel is able to direct a flow right down into your heart. God is up in heaven, tipping this big bucket of love your way and it is just pouring right down into your heart by the Holy Spirit. God wants to do this for you now. Believe it! He wants to do it because these are the experiences that revolutionize our lives. You don't learn everything *intellectually* by listening to cerebral lectures, but *experientially* when the love of God touches you. Most people are smart enough to know when they are in love. God wants to dump a barrel of love down into your heart by the Holy Spirit. When that happens to you, you will know about it. Despite all your brokenness and weakness and failure and everything else, you will know that the love of God is the primary thing.

Paul said that hope doesn't disappoint us. We need not be disappointed when things in life don't go the way we thought, because the love of God has been poured into our hearts by the Holy Spirit.

The communion meal is one of the greatest symbols of God's love for us. Through communion, of course we are remembering the Lord's death until He comes, and we are remembering what happened on the cross, but we are also so aware of God's love. We are remembering what Jesus did for us on the cross because of *the very fact of God's love*. God so loved our world that He sacrificed His only begotten Son. Jesus Himself chose to love us more than He loved Himself. His love overcame every barrier – losing His reputation, enduring great suffering and pain, and all while we were still sinners.

Jesus wants you to know His love more than

anything else. That is why He was prepared to go to the cross to pay your outstanding debts. He cancelled your sin so that by faith in Him you could come before God and receive His forgiveness and salvation. I often say to people, "God loves you." Simply that. "God loves you." He loves you just the way you are. You don't have to do one thing. Even with all your sin, shame, brokenness and failures – yes, He loves you just the way you are. Even if you are a seasoned Christian that has done many things for God and you are full of the Spirit and you have a ministry, of course He loves you too, but He doesn't love you any more today than the day He saved you. He loves you just the way you are too. However, He loves all of us too much to leave us the way we are. He doesn't want us to continue living life being hurt by sin and disappointed by failure. He calls us into *life* and *holiness*, and He calls us into *freedom* and into *relationship* with Him. This is the love of God that has been poured out in your heart.

Nothing can separate us from God's love

John 3:16, perhaps the most outstanding verse in the Bible, sums up God's love for us. God loved us enough to sacrifice the life of His only Son so that we should not perish, but instead gain everlasting life. Why did He do it? Because He loved you. Why would the Father ask Jesus to submit to murderous hands and die in shame before an angry mob? Simply because of an amazing love, far beyond our understanding.

Romans 8:35 reminds us of His love again: *"Who shall separate us from the love of Christ?"* Do you have faith in His love for you? The evidence of Scripture is overwhelming. I am not worried about the devil and what he is planning; the traps he is setting and the destruction that he wants to do, because I have faith in the overcoming love of God. You don't need to be anxious or worried about anything when you know that your heavenly Father is watching over you.

Have faith in the love of God – a childlike faith. Lean on Him and acknowledge His love. Many times fears will assail you and the enemy will rise up, but nevertheless have faith in His love. He will never fail you.

It is always amazing to see how confident kids become when they know their parents are with them. Whereas before they may have been shy or quiet, they will act very differently when father or mother are around. Suddenly they can talk tough; they can do all kinds of things because they know they've got some back-up behind them. It's the same for us. When there is danger around or we are uncertain, or afraid, we must lean on Jesus.

Romans 8:35 goes on to list a number of things – none of which, bad as they may be, will be able to take God's love away from us: tribulation, distress, persecution, famine, nakedness, peril or the sword. None of these things need destroy us because of God's great love for us.

God is love

Paul concludes that, even though all these things may assail us, we are, "*... more than conquerors through him who loved us*" (Romans 8:37). But then he goes on to say an even more amazing thing:

> "*For I am convinced that neither death nor life, neither angels nor demons, neither the present nor the future, nor any powers, neither height nor depth, nor anything else in all creation, will be able to separate us from the love of God that is in Christ Jesus our Lord.*"
> (Romans 8:38–39)

How amazing! No supernatural force, not even death itself will separate us from God's love. God *is* love. It is more than just a commodity, it is *who He is*. If there is one word that sums up His nature, it's the word *love* – the agapé love of God; the benevolent, all-caring, all-wise, all-providing, all-passionate, all-encompassing love of God. That is the foundation of your faith and that is why you should have faith in the love of God – because you are standing upon the very substance of who God is.

Aren't you glad that God's basic, foundational character trait is love? Imagine if He was more concerned about justice, or more concerned about getting the job done, or more concerned about straightening you out than He was in loving you?

"*... we know and rely on the love God has for us. God*

is love. Whoever lives in love lives in God, and God in him."   (1 John 4:16)

This great love of God does not just give us a warm, fuzzy feeling. God loves us in a real, practical way. The penultimate verse of the book of Jude reads,

"To him who is able to keep you from falling and to present you before his glorious presence without fault and with great joy . . ."   (Jude 24)

So we see that God's love is not just aimed at you, it *surrounds* you. God wants to wrap His arms around you and keep you safe. When you have faith in His love and power, then He is able to keep you from falling. When you have faith in His love He is able to shape you and guide you, so as to ultimately present you faultless before the presence of His glory with exceeding joy.

You are valuable

In Matthew 10:26–31 Jesus advised His disciples never to worry about anything. He urged them not to spend time worrying about those who hated them and wanted to destroy them.

" . . . even the very hairs of your head are all numbered. So don't be afraid . . ."   (Matthew 10:29)

Jesus told them that God knew when even the smallest sparrow fell to the ground, and that they were much more valuable to God. God knows all about you – even the number of hairs on your head. Think about the implications of that statement. Jesus was not using hyperbole. He was not exaggerating for the sake of making a point. His statement is literally true. God is so wise, so incredibly intelligent and capable, that He is able to take a running total on the number of hairs on the heads of all His children simultaneously! He is big enough to keep track of everything. He is very, very thorough and very, very capable. He is also love incarnate. What a combination!

Think about any issues that are in your heart right now, that you are worrying about, or are nervous about. Take those issues to God and place them in His hands today. We don't often think of worry as a sin, but the Bible says it is. When fear takes hold of you and you begin to get concerned about things, it's easy to stop trusting God for everything. But you shouldn't worry, because God knows all about the issues that are occupying your mind. He holds your very next breath is in His hand! If He has taken the trouble to count the hairs on your head, then you have reason to trust in His love for you. God is more than equal to the task of meeting your needs and dealing with the issues in your life. Trust in Him. Jesus said, "I will never leave you or forsake you." Begin to lean into the love of God.

3. You can have faith in His presence

We need to have faith in God's Word, faith in His love for us, and we can also put our faith in His *presence.* Faith in God is not just an intellectual exercise. God's presence is real and tangible. His presence and power are demonstrations of His being. When the presence of God shows up, lives are changed and people's faith level is lifted.

It never ceases to amaze me in healing meetings, that as one or two people begin to get healed of something, faith rises in others in the meeting. People think, "Wow, maybe God will touch me too." That is what happens when His presence is manifest. It is easier for you to put your faith in Him when you see His power and presence manifest.

I love this statement of Paul's in 1 Corinthians:

"My message and my preaching were not with wise and persuasive words, but with a demonstration of the Spirit's power, so that your faith might not rest on men's wisdom, but on God's power."

(1 Corinthians 2:5)

Paul didn't put together a persuasive sermon that would convince his listeners. Although he was highly-educated and a gifted communicator, he chose not to use clever words. Instead He relied upon a demonstration of the power of the Holy Spirit, so that those who became believers would have the power of God as the foundation of their faith. People hunger for an authentic experience of the power and presence of God. When people are filled with His presence and power it initiates a life-changing process in the heart which is transformational. It enables you to put your trust in Him like never before. Paul said that is why Jesus came performing signs and wonders, so that people would have a demonstration of Emmanuel – God with us – that they could put their faith and confidence in.

Jesus said to those who were struggling to put their faith in Him, "Look, if you don't believe what I'm telling you, at least believe what you see with your own eyes – the lame walk, the blind see and the deaf hear!"

We should never try to demand God's presence and power. We won't experience His presence by trying to force God to show up. This type of approach will turn you into an aggressive striver who is forever trying to press in and grasp what you want from God. It doesn't work that way. Striving is human effort, and human effort leads to legalism. But the Bible teaches that we enter God's presence with thanksgiving and praise. We express our love and thanks to Him and worship Him. When we do that, God is delighted to reveal Himself to us and bless us.

Expect God's presence
If thanksgiving is a key to God's presence, then you

need to cultivate an attitude of thankfulness. All of us have so much to be thankful for. You can begin to thank God for things past and present, and also for what He will do in the future. Sometimes people are afraid to expect God to move in power – in case He doesn't! This is the wrong attitude to have. Be expectant of God always. Being afraid that God won't show up when you most need Him is almost like a curse. According to your faith, so be it! If you don't think something will happen then it probably won't.

Expectancy is a key to seeing God move. When you purpose to believe, God is faithful. When you trust in Him, secure in the knowledge of His great power, then you can begin to call forth those things that you believe God has promised you, that don't yet exist, as though they did. You can begin to say, "Thank you Lord for healed marriages. Thank you Lord for saved children. Thank you Lord for your provision. Thank you Lord for your anointing. Thank you Lord that underneath me are Your everlasting arms. Thank you that You see every aspect of my life." Let His praise be continually in your mouth.

Listen to the voice of the Holy Spirit. Listen to the One who knows all about you; the One who knows the number of hairs on your head; the One who loves you enough to die for you. Listen to His voice calling you saying, *"Come to me, all you who are weary and burdened, and I will give you rest"* (Matthew 11:28).

Jesus wants to bring you into the fullness of all that the Father has purposed for your life. The Father says to you today, "Put your faith in My word, in My love and in My presence. For I am faithful." Amen.

If you have enjoyed this book and would like to help us to send a copy of it and many other titles to needy pastors in the **Third World**, please write for further information or send your gift to:

Sovereign World Trust
PO Box 777, Tonbridge
Kent TN11 0ZS
United Kingdom

or to the **'Sovereign World'** distributor in your country.

Visit our website at **www.sovereign-world.org**
for a full range of Sovereign World books.